With happy memories of your
brief visit.
The Smith Family.
John   Tina.
Beth   Owen.

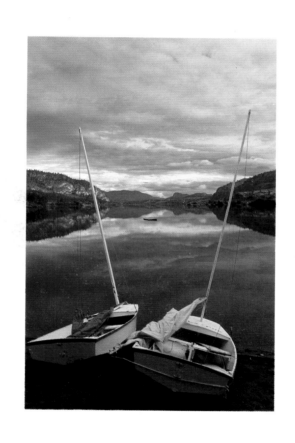

BRITISH C

This edition published by
Whitecap Books Ltd.
1086 West Third Street
North Vancouver, B.C.
Canada V7P 3J6

Produced by
Bison Books Corp.
15 Sherwood Place
Greenwich, CT 06830
USA

ISBN 0-921061-04-8

Printed in Hong Kong

Reprinted 1988

OLUMBIA

TEXT	ROBIN LANGLEY SOMMER
DESIGN	MIKE ROSE
PHOTOGRAPHY	PHOTO/GRAPHICS STOCK LIBRARY

Whitecap Books
NORTH VANCOUVER, B.C., CANADA

 A Bison Book

PHOTO CREDITS

Photo on page 24 courtesy of Parks Canada (W Lynch).

Photo/Graphics Stock Library, North Vancouver, British Columbia:
D & J Abson: 49, 69, 77, 92-93; C Angus: 22-23, 42 top; J Brouwer: 17;
M Burch: 21 bottom, 36, 40-41, 44-45, 68, 94; J R A Burridge: 78-79, 116-117,
119; F Chapman: 48, 83, 91, 99, 112-113, 124-125; B Herger: 1,
20, 26-27, 55, 59, 60-61, 64, 66-67, 80, 86-87, 90, 95, 96-97,
98, 104-105, 102, 107; R W Laurilla: 82 top right and bottom left,
88-89, 100-101, 103 bottom, 103 top; R Marotz: 15, 16, 21 top, 47, 62-63, 81,
126; G Marx: 25, 29, 30, 33, 43 bottom, 52-53, 57, 65, 73, 76, 82 top left
and bottom right, 85, 111 bottom, 108-109, 115, 122 top right, 123, 128;
V Matisic: 75; G Maurer: 70-71, 120-121; P Morrow: 118;
M Petkov: 3-6, 31, 34-35, 37, 38-39, 54; M Robertson: 28;
J Vogt: 43 top, 46 (both), 50 (both), 51, 56, 72, 74, 122 bottom right;
G Wedmark: 18-19; T Willis: 122 top and bottom left; R Wright:
110, 111 top, 114, 127.

3-6 *The Vancouver skyline at night.*

INTRODUCTION

British Columbians are justifiably proud and protective of their water-born, mountain-bred land, Canada's only province on the Pacific Ocean. That pride is reflected in their provincial motto, *Splendor Sine Occasu*—Splendor Without Diminishment. Separated from most of their fellow Canadians by peaks and plains, British Columbians look to the Pacific rather than toward the St Lawrence. Many of them have come here by that ocean route, from China, Japan and other Asian countries; some came originally from Italy, Greece and Eastern Europe, or from the eastern part of Canada. Like Americans of the West, British Columbians are a pioneering people who reflect their heritage in an independent, open-minded spirit. Characteristically, they are energetic, democratic and amenable to change, provided it be change for the better.

Other Canadians tend to regard British Columbians as a special breed capable of almost anything—a reputation enhanced by such unique provincial activities as the annual powered bathtub race across the Strait of Georgia. It began as a joke in 1967, and the joke has gotten bigger every year as more bathtubbers strive to finish the course in an upright position. That's about the only prize, except for a hilariously good time.

Historically, visitors to British Columbia have been drawn first to the scenic provincial capital of Victoria, on Vancouver Island, and to the nearby mainland city of Vancouver, which has a multitude of attractions, from its setting of rare natural beauty to its international cuisine. Vancouver's population is well over a million, of which more than half is of non-British origin.

The busiest Pacific port of the Americas, Vancouver is also one of the 12 major ports of the world. Burrard Inlet has been called 'the city's most important business street,' as its freighters, liners and ferries bustle in and out of the strait laden with passengers, forest products, coal and grain. Millions of tons of Canadian exports pass through this gateway to the Orient every year, as a result of Vancouver's favorable location, which made it the western terminus of the Canadian Pacific Railway in 1885. Since then the city has prospered, and gleaming steel-and-glass skyscrapers have replaced the sawmill settlement that stood here a century ago.

But commerce and industry are not the whole story of Vancouver, which remains closely attuned to nature and to human needs beyond the material. Thousand-acre Stanley Park occupies the peninsula between English Bay and Burrard Inlet, offering both extensive sandy beaches and hiking trails shadowed by soaring Western red cedar and other beautiful trees and flowering shrubs. Picnic grounds, flower gardens, cricket fields, the children's zoo and an outstanding aquarium are other attractions. Little Mountain, once a stone quarry site, has been transformed into the splendid Queen Elizabeth Park by skillful landscaping, including the creation of a sunken garden of unusual beauty. Nearby Grouse Mountain offers skiing with a panoramic view of the city below.

At night, Vancouver sparkles with lights and laughter. Summer brings thousands of luxury cruise-ship passengers ashore to throng Granville Street, Gastown and Chinatown. Theater, symphony and a marvelously varied cuisine add to the excitement of Canada's third largest city.

Easily accessible from the mainland by ferry, float plane and other craft are historic Vancouver Island and the Gulf Islands of the Strait of Georgia. The many small islands along the southern coast enjoy mild weather, pastoral scenery and an unhurried way of life; they are popular vacation and fishing retreats. Vancouver Island, 282 miles long, is the largest in the western Americas and played an important role in all the exploratory activity that focused on the Northwest. The island is named for British explorer George Vancouver, who charted the Pacific coast of Canada in 1792, 14 years after Captain James Cook put in at Nootka Sound on the island's west coast. He was well received by the Nootka Indians, and news of his expedition brought both British and Americans into the sea-otter fur trade, which the Russians had dominated since the ill-fated Bering expedition of 1741. Sea-otter pelts were in great demand, particularly in China, where they were considered the most beautiful and valuable of furs, and a lucrative trade was carried on throughout the nineteenth century.

Today, lumber and agriculture are the island's most important industries and its major city is Victoria, the provincial capital, which was established as a trading post of the Hudson's Bay Company in 1843. Though half a world away from England, Victoria retains its colonial-capital ambience. The majestic Empress Hotel on Government Street, along with the handsome Parliament buildings, presides over the scenic Inner Harbour. Tweeds, chinaware and woolen goods are much in evidence in the downtown shops, and gardening is highly esteemed. Nearby Butchart Gardens, a floral wonderland created from a former lime quarry, draws thousands of visitors every year. The city's street lamps are adorned with hanging baskets of flowers, and numerous birds are fed, protected and observed in three shoreline sanctuaries and in Beacon Hill Park, where majestic white swans and innumerable colorful ducks come and go. Numerous boats of every kind testify to Victoria's maritime history.

British Columbia's population is heaviest in the Vancouver/Victoria coastal region; much of the province is still wilderness, and the cities and farms east of the Coast Mountains are often widely scattered. Northeastern British Columbia is a section of the Great Plains of North America, formed by sediments that were once at the bottom of ancient seas and freshwater lakes. The rest of the province is part of the massive chain of mountains that extends from Alaska to the tip of South America—the Cordillera, as the Spanish called it. Within the province, which is Canada's third largest, three main groups of mountains determine the contours of the land. In the West are the Coast Mountains and the large offshore islands that once lay beneath the Pacific. Now they form a protective chain that shelters the Inside Passage to Alaska. In the East are the 50-million-year-old Rockies, dramatically affected by erosion as a result of their great height. The interior mountains, including the Purcells, Selkirks, Monashees and Cariboos, are older than the Rockies but less severely eroded, because they were not lifted so high by the volcanic forces that formed them.

The mountains help govern British Columbia's climate, which is very mild on the Pacific Coast, where the Japanese Current, or Kuroshio, prevails. As successive mountain ranges block moist air moving inland from the Pacific, there is a pattern of heavy precipitation on the western slopes and sunny, drier conditions on the eastern side. These variations affect the many kinds of plant and animal life that abound in the province, while altitude plays an important role as well. The treeline gradually drops from south to north, where trees grow slowly because the soil thaws for only short periods of the summer.

Forest still covers some 60 percent of the province, providing not only its major source of revenue, but a congenial home for native wildlife including grizzly and black bears, cougar, and mountain sheep and goats. Moose have extended their range far south of their former limits around the northerly Prince George region; as a result of lumbering operations opening up the forest, they now approach the Canadian-US border. Migratory waterfowl including black brants, Canada and snow geese, swans and brightly plumaged ducks make their summer homes here. There are numerous game birds and fish, including the Pacific salmon that penetrate deeply into the coastal inlets and rivers to reach their spawning grounds. Along the coastline, herring and halibut help keep the province's long-time fishing industry prosperous.

This is a country of water and woods, where the mighty Columbia River and the hasty Fraser spring up in the Rocky Mountain trench and pursue their separate ways to the sea. The Thompson rises in the Cariboo Mountains and joins the Fraser at Lytton. The northern rivers of the Mackenzie system, including the Liard and the Peace, flow eastward. There are also hundreds of beautiful lakes, including Kootenay, Atlin, Stuart and those of the Okanagan Valley.

Unlike the rugged Kootenay region, the Okanagan is sheltered, calm and fertile now that its waterways are used to irrigate rich farms and orchards.

The valley is an important source of both food and wine made from its famous grapes. Valuable fruit tree crops are raised in the southern interior, and black and white Holstein cattle graze in the pastures here.

Canada's beef industry began during the Gold Rush, when US cattle were driven to the Cariboo to supply the prospectors. The Cariboo and Kamloops regions of the interior still have British Columbia's biggest ranches, while the northern Peace River district produces grain. Mining, natural gas and petroleum are other important sectors of the economy. One of the fastest-growing industries is tourism: steadily increasing numbers of visitors from other parts of Canada and the world are discovering British Columbia's unique combination of natural beauty and a relaxed way of life in which to enjoy it.

Five national parks and more than 300 provincial parks provide for every recreational need. Pacific Rim, a marine park on western Vancouver Island, centers on beautiful Long Beach—one of British Columbia's few stretches of sandy shoreline—and takes in many of the smaller islands. Mountainous parks include Yoho and Kootenay in the Rockies, which share common boundaries with each other and with Alberta's Banff National Park. Glacier National Park, in the Selkirk and Purcell Mountains, contains more than a hundred spectacular rivers of ice. Majestic Mount Revelstoke, in the Selkirks, is flanked by the Monashees, a popular ski area. Trail-riding, backpacking, canoeing, camping and fishing are other popular sports in these beautiful alpine and subalpine wilderness areas. Living history is found at Barkerville in the Cariboo, recently restored to its Gold-Rush-days appearance, and mineral hot springs make Kootenay National Park a popular health spa. Wherever one goes in British Columbia—coast or interior, Southwest or North—one can expect to meet a congenial people proud of their heritage and the natural wonders that remain unspoiled.

Robin Langley Sommer

VANCOUVER ISLAND AND THE GULF ISLANDS

Spanish, Russian and British mariners had explored the north Pacific coast for more than two centuries by the time that Captain George Vancouver claimed Vancouver Island for England in 1792. But this largest island in the western Americas (over 12,000 square miles in area) had no permanent settlement by Europeans until 1843, when Fort Victoria was set up on behalf of the Hudson's Bay Company. At first, temporary settlement centered around the sea otter trade, but during the late nineteenth century farms and sawmills were operating around Victoria, Alberni, Nanaimo and other towns. Agriculture and lumber are still important industries on the island.

Long summers, cloudless skies and Canada's most moderate climate make Vancouver Island desirable either as a vacation resort or a place of permanent residence. The pace of life is slow here, and plentiful parklands provide a variety of outdoor activities. Scenic Pacific Rim National Park protects three unique areas on the west coast—ocean beach, rain forest and coastal islands. The West Coast Trail—a rugged five-day hike, for those who really want to get away—follows the island's coastline through dense rain forest.

Vancouver Island's population is concentrated in the south and along the east coast. At the southernmost tip of the island is the sedate and gracious maritime city of Victoria, British Columbia's provincial capital. The Empress Hotel, on the waterfront, is still Victoria's best-known landmark, and visitors flock to take tea in its spacious lobby every afternoon. The city's distinctly English air is due mainly to the fact that Victoria's exceptional climate and former colonial status attracted many retired colonial administrators from India and the Far East. Here they could afford to live on a much grander scale than in Britain, and the city's atmosphere was one that the old 'China hands' found congenial and to which they contributed a tone of elegant gentility. That remains today, along with the London style doubler-decker buses, horse-drawn 'tallyhos' and three castles, one of which is now Royal Roads Military College. History buffs are attracted to the excellent provincial archives, housed next to the Parliament buildings, and nearby Thunderbird Park, whose totem poles recall the island's native people and their legends. The most notable of many popular gardens is Butchart Gardens, 17 miles north of Victoria on Saanich Peninsula. It is a floral wonderland, created from a lime quarry that operated during the early 1900s, and draws thousands of admiring visitors a year. North of Victoria, all the way to wild Cape Scott Park at the other end of the island, there are innumerable coves and inlets, lakes and rivers to explore at an unhurried pace.

Fifteen major islands comprise the Gulf Islands, off the southeast end of Vancouver Island. Indians called the largest the Saltspring Chuan, or 'facing the sea.' They believed that the island's smooth summits were landing places for the great Swaquaw, the Thunderbird, which created thunder with its mighty wings and shot lightning bolts from its eyes. The Swaquaw seized whales from the waves and carried them to mountain tops, where it devoured them. More prosaically, early white settlers called Saltspring Admiral Island, but they changed the name when the island's salt deposits became economically important. Gulf Island towns are simple and pleasant, closely attuned to the sea and dependent upon ferries and other craft for communication with the larger world. Wildflowers grow profusely, and deer often browse among the cattle and sheep in open pastures. Small homes are tucked away among the woods and fields, and those who vacation here return again and again. Those who live here rarely leave for long.

15 Peaceful Hornby Island is a haven from the hurried pace of urban life. Winters here are mild enough for long walks on the beach.

16 Backed by Vancouver Island's MacKenzie Range, the fishing town of Tofino is a popular resort.

17 An impressive catch is displayed with pride by fishermen of the waters around Vancouver Island.

18-19 A British Columbia ferry threads its way through the Gulf Islands between Vancouver Island and the mainland.

20 Mother and daughter send their kite soaring
aloft in the breezes off Vancouver Island.

21 top Vancouver Island contains many stands of
older Douglas firs. This giant is known as the Red
Creek Fir and is the largest tree in Canada.

21 bottom Boating is a way of life at Gambier
Island in Howe Sound.

22-23 Sailboats out of Vancouver take full
advantage of the 4400 miles of coastline afforded
by British Columbia's numerous islands.

24 Sea lions gather at Pacific Rim National Park,
whose waters support a multitude of seabirds and
mammals, including the gray whale.

25 Sunset over Long Beach at low tide, when the restless motion of the great rollers is stilled for a time.

26-27 A solitary boatman is silhouetted by the setting sun, emblem of British Columbia.

30 *A tranquil view across the Inner Harbour.*

31 *Victoria's illuminated Legislative Building (1898) is an impressive sight for mariners entering the Inner Harbour by night.*

VANCOUVER

Vancouver has been described as the only city where a person can play golf and ski in the same day and still have time to dine out and attend the symphony at night. Metropolitan Vancouver is Canada's third largest city, and the pulse and commercial hub of British Columbia. Nine municipalities comprise the 350-square-mile community.

Vancouver's commercial authority derives from its role as the rail-sea nexus of Canada. When the Canadian Pacific Railway selected Burrard Inlet as its western terminus a hundred years ago, Vancouver's future was assured. The former backwater made rapid strides in population and construction, as the railroad built wharves to serve ships sailing to and from the Far East. The opening of the Panama Canal in 1914 could only increase Vancouver's traffic by providing an easy sea-route to Europe, and a year later a second transcontinental railroad reached the city. Since then the port has expanded steadily to challenge and then surpass its former rivals in Canada and the United States: Victoria, Prince Rupert, Seattle and San Francisco.

Travelers entering Vancouver by sea pass under the welcoming arch of the soaring Lions Gate suspension bridge over Burrard Inlet into one of the world's most beautiful harbours. They step ashore into the heart of the city's thriving business district, surrounded by handsome highrise buildings with views of the inlet and the mountains that overlook it. On the opposite shore is North Vancouver, accessible by sea-bus.

For many visitors, the city's restaurants are a major attraction, offering cuisines from around the world. In Gastown, where Vancouver began, a bold approach to urban renewal has rescued many of the city's historic buildings from the wrecker's ball and refurbished them to house restaurants, discos, boutiques and art galleries. Neat brick walkways, traditional streetlamps and a tall steam clock whose whistles mark the hours contribute to the neighborhood's charm.

Another area that is popular with Vancouverites and visitors alike is Chinatown, which originated in the 1880s when many Chinese were brought into British Columbia to work on railroad construction. At first resented and often harassed, those Chinese who made Vancouver their home gradually won general respect and admiration for their many contributions to the community. Many Chinese Canadians no longer live in Chinatown, but the region remains a vital cultural center and the source of many exotic goods: camphorwood, jade, ivory, silk and bamboo. Chinatown's excellent restaurants feature almost every major Chinese cuisine, including Szechuan, Peking or Mandarin, Cantonese, Hunan and Shanghai. Games of mahjong are still a favorite leisure pastime.

Vancouver's beautiful natural setting provides attractions that draw people from all over the world. Nearby Grouse Mountain with its cable cars offers opportunities for a panoramic view of the city, as well as skiing facilities. Stanley Park with its beaches, woodlands and Canada's foremost aquarium, and the world's longest suspension footbridge over the Capilano River in North Vancouver are just two more of many outdoors attractions. The city combines genial livability and hospitality with a wealth of cultural and recreational activities. As Canada's gateway to the Pacific, Vancouver is a city of many countries, and its diverse people have a way of making their dreams come true.

33 Vancouver's harbour handles most of Canada's industrial exports to Japan, Brazil, South Korea and other lands. It is an even busier port than San Francisco.

34-35 View from the top of Vancouver's innovative courthouse, looking past the Art Gallery and downtown buildings to the mountains of the North Shore.

36 Downtown Vancouver from the Pan Pacific Hotel, one of many elegant hostelries with an international guest list.

37 Popular Gastown is an historic re-creation of early Vancouver on Water Street, near the harbour. It is named for Jack 'Gassy' Deighton, an early adventurer known for his tall tales.

38-39 The impressive steel and glass towers of downtown Vancouver form a grid of progress.

40/41 Canada Harbour Place, a multi-tiered complex on the waterfront, seems ready to set sail.

42 top Pleasure boats mingle with shipping containers loaded with bulk cargo in Vancouver's False Creek.

42 bottom British Columbia's judiciary has its headquarters in Vancouver rather than Victoria.

43 A luxurious cruise ship departs Burrard Inlet under the Lions Gate Bridge.

44-45 Lighthouse Park, in West Vancouver.

46 Vancouver's exciting Chinatown attracts visitors from around the world to sample its incomparable food and exotic treasures of ivory, jade and silk.

47 Vancouver's Chinese community—the largest in North America after San Francisco's—celebrates Canada Day.

48 *Beautiful Queen Elizabeth Park occupies the highest point of land within Vancouver city limits.*

49 Families of Canada geese stop spring traffic around Stanley Park when they stroll across nearby streets.

50 Granville Island is a thriving marketplace opposite the city's gleaming downtown area.

51 Fresh produce from the Fraser and Okanagan Valleys is in demand at the Granville Island market.

52-53 *Colorful annuals in Stanley Park flourish in Vancouver's mild climate.*

54 *A graceful bridge arches over a waterway under snow-laden trees in Stanley Park.*

55 *The park is equally beautiful in the spring rain, with its flowering trees in blossom.*

56-57 *Marine life at Vancouver's aquarium, one of the world's best, includes sharks, alligators, and beluga and killer whales.*

THE SOUTHWEST

British Columbia's southwestern region has more than half the province's people, concentrated around Vancouver, Burnaby, Richmond and New Westminster. Many more live in the Fraser Valley. The lower valley is not only beautiful but fertile: much of the region's food is grown in this six-million-acre expanse between East Vancouver and Hope. The Fraser River, British Columbia's longest, is tempered on its approach to the valley; its northeastern course is rugged and downright dangerous, as explorer Simon Fraser found out to his cost. But in the flatlands west of Hope, the great river makes its final descent into the Strait of Georgia at New Westminster. Here the turbulent stream that cut the Fraser Canyon to the north widens to a smooth, powerful river flanked by a fertile valley.

The silt-laden river feeds the rich soil of the valley but it can also be destructive during spring flooding. Today floods are largely controlled and the river and the mild climate combine to keep the valley lush and green all year. In this pastoral setting, horseback riding, fishing and country fairs are all part of the way of life.

Closer to Vancouver are several extensive provincial parks that carry city dwellers back to nature in a matter of hours. Hikers and skiers frequent Mount Seymour, which offers a breathtaking view of thousands of acres of lakes and forests. Five-thousand-foot Mount Bishop is the highest point in the park. Garibaldi Provincial Park takes in over half a million wilderness acres in the Coastal Range. Visitors to the Diamond Head area in spring will find vast carpets of heather and alpine flowers below the 7000-foot Diamond Head peak, an extinct volcano ringed by natural sculptures of lava. Sapphire-blue Garibaldi Lake, as seen from Panorama Ridge, is a scene well worth the half-day's hiking required to view it. In the Black Tusk area, a great nature conservancy protects the native wildflowers, heathers and shrubs, and there are numerous glaciers, including Sentinel, Sphinx and Helm. Snow remains in the high places here until well into July.

Wildlife lovers will have a hard time seeing the black and grizzly bears that inhabit the park; they shy away from human contact. More accessible are the deer that forage in the underbrush, and the marmots that sunbathe on the rocks and emit their piercing whistles of warning when alarmed. Ptarmigan allow humans a fairly close approach before they break cover in a burst of feathered energy, and the bold Canada jay is likely to be a constant companion. Mountain goats may be spied on their high, rocky lookouts, and the golden eagle frequents these regions. Cars are not permitted into the park, so the wilderness remains unspoiled, visited mainly by hardy seekers of nature who are willing to brave Garialdi's canyons, gulleys, mountainsides and crater walls.

Nearby Whistler Mountain, on the contrary, has been created expressly as a resort area from the town formerly known as Alta Lake. British Columbia Rail regularly delivers skiers who swear that there is no other place for them than Whistler's thousand square miles of beautiful slopes. Named for the thousands of marmots who greeted early explorers with their whistling call, the mountain now resounds to the calls of snow and glacier skiers who return again and again to enjoy the area's incomparable facilities.

59 British Columbia's lower west coast has many peaceful inlets and flower-dotted marshlands.

60-61 Beautiful Garibaldi Lake, located just a short drive north of Vancouver, is a popular hiking destination.

62-63 *Gemlike Stave Lake is typical of the many beautiful lakes of southwestern British Columbia.*

64 *Canoeing is a popular pastime with visitors to the scenic river valleys of the southwest.*

65 *Powell River began as a logging and fishing center and holds to its maritime tradition with an annual Sea Fair Week that packs the harbour.*

66-67 *Pacific salmon are an important part of the traditional fisherman's way of life here.*

68 *A sunbather enjoys Nairn Falls Park, on the Green River near Pemberton Meadows.*

69 *Adventurous whitewater rafters challenge the rapids of the Fraser Canyon.*

70-71 *Cross-country skiing in Mount Seymour Provincial Park, nine miles from downtown Vancouver.*

72 The Coast Mountains, often wreathed in mist,
recede to the horizon.

73 Black Tusk rises over 7000 feet in scenic
Garibaldi Provincial Park north of Vancouver.

74 *Enjoying an aerial view of Mount Seymour and its rugged setting of over 8000 wilderness acres.*

75 *Whistler Mountain's attractive ski resorts give access to 1000 square miles of spectacular slopes.*

76 Haunting moonlit evergreens clothed in snow cling to life along the treeline.

77 The aptly named Elfin Lakes of Garibaldi Provincial Park evoke a feeling of Switzerland.

78-79 *The mild climate of southwestern British Columbia makes it one of the province's prime agricultural regions.*

80 *The lower Fraser Valley, six million acres in area, is highly productive farmland which benefits from a mild climate.*

81 The beautiful waterways of British Columbia's Pacific Coast are thoroughfares for the logging industry.

82 Some of the many species of Canadian wildlife indigenous to British Columbia are (clockwise from top left): the ground squirrel, the common flicker, the ring-necked pheasant, and the red-tailed hawk.

83 Aspen trees in shimmering fall foliage—the Bottanie Valley.

THE INTERIOR

The communities of British Columbia's interior are as clearly defined as the geographic features that gave rise to them. In the southeast, the East and West Kootenays comprise an area twice as large as Switzerland. In this rugged landscape the towns grew up in isolation from each other. Kimberley, Canada's highest town, began as a base-metals mining center and has recently been transformed into a Bavarian-style village. Revelstoke was a CPR construction camp in its early days; now it is a flourishing resort community that serves two nearby national parks.

In contrast to the high country of the Kootenays, the Okanagan region west of them is sheltered, calm and fertile. Water from the many lakes and rivers is used to irrigate farms and orchards, making this area an essential part of the provincial economy: only three percent of British Columbia's land is suitable for agriculture.

The first settlers of the Okanagan Valley raised cattle and grain, but from the 1890s on, many grew fruit instead. They shipped it to market by shallow-draft sternwheelers that took advantage of their many waterways. Now these tree-fruit crops are the most valuable grown in British Columbia. Names like Peachland and Summerland attest to the valley's mild climate and pleasant way of life.

Penticton, in the heart of the Okanagan, was a ranch in the 1860s, and Salmon Arm, at the head of the valley, is the gateway to cattle country. Kamloops, capital of the southern interior, was established as a fur-trading post in 1812 but became a well-known railroad and meat-packing center. To the west, Merritt thrives on a combination of lumber and livestock, augmented by molybdenum from a nearby mine.

The Cariboo constitutes a more than 20,000-square-mile territory in central southeast British Columbia, which allegedly got its name when miners of the gold-rush days associated the region with the caribou. Somehow the 'u' got lost, but the area remains an outdoorsman's paradise, where fishing and hunting are among the best on the continent. In spring the Cariboo is filled with the scent of wild roses, lupines and sweet-smelling grasses, and big game animals abound. Its Blue River is near the northern entrance to Wells Gray Provincial Park—almost two million acres of untamed wilderness. Here hikers can choose among several trails, including Battle Mountain and Trophy Mountain, that traverse a country composed of snowfields, glaciers, mineral springs and alpine meadows. As almost everywhere in British Columbia, boating is a major means of both transportation and recreation. A host of ghost towns hold memories of the gold-rush years.

The highway north of Williams Lake leads to Prince George, which is close to the geographic center of British Columbia. The city's site was selected by Simon Fraser in 1807 as a fur-trading post at the junction of the Nechako and Fraser Rivers. Now it is the chief distribution center for this part of the country. Prince George has numerous pulp mills and sawmills, and forest industries are a mainstay of more northern communities as well, such as Prince Rupert, Vanderhoof and Burns Lake. The frontier spirit remains alive in the interior, which is experiencing steady growth in the areas of logging, ranching, mining and tourism.

85 Vernon's lovely setting in the Okanagan makes it an extremely popular resort community.

86-87 Snowfields and glaciers mark Mount Revelstoke National Park; the mountain's lower slopes have an annual snowfall of some 20-30 feet.

88-89 *Much of the British Columbian interior is
still pioneer country.*

90 *Tall sunflowers grace a farm near Grand Forks,
settled by Doukhobors of Russian ancestry at the
turn of the century.*

91 Most of British Columbia's rich vineyards are located between Kelowna and Osoyoos; 90 percent of their crops go to local wineries.

92-93 Sun-filled Summerland, in the Kelowna region, has excellent lake views and popular resorts.

94 An idyllic scene near Princeton: the hills here form the western flank of the Cascades.

95 A gossamer web of jewels overhangs a misty lake by the first light of day.

96-97 A solitary angler is out early to try his luck in a glass-like pond.

98 *The pure white flower of the dogwood tree is British Columbia's provincial flower.*

99 *A flowering orchard holds one spellbound in the Okanagan country.*

100-101 *Skiers tour the white immensity of the Battle Range.*

102 A warm holiday welcome is promised by this home in Salmon Arm, near Shuswap Lake.

103 top A triumphant climber surveys the Melville Group in the Battle Range, near Selkirk.

103 bottom Heli-skiing in the Monashees, where winter sports are a way of life.

104/105 The minute shelters of wilderness-seeking campers are almost lost in the sweeping vistas that surround them.

THE NORTH

From Prince George, it is almost 500 miles to Prince Rupert on the Pacific Coast. Nor'wester Simon Fraser was the first white man to visit this territory, which he called New Caledonia because it reminded him of his mother's highland birthplace in Scotland. Toward the coast, over 100 inches of annual rainfall is the norm, and the summers are quite cool. Fishing dominates logging in the coastal areas, and Prince Rupert is the home port of a large commercial fleet that depends on salmon, halibut, cod, shrimp, oyster and other species plentiful in northern waters.

Some 50 miles across the Hecate Strait from Prince Rupert lie the remote Queen Charlotte Islands. Their rocky coastlines defied the landing attempts of the first mariners but their population is growing now as a result of mining, petroleum, logging and other activities. The Haidas were the first occupants here: they roamed the Pacific coastline as far south as California in 60-man dugout canoes, making war and taking slaves from other native peoples. But their ranks were severely depleted by smallpox and syphilis when the white people came; only recently have they begun to recover. Their name for the more than 150 islands that comprise the group could be translated roughly as 'The house is open and ready for you.' Migratory birds seem to respond to this invitation, as their nesting and resting sites cover the islands. Naturalists find other phenomena of unusual interest here too. For example, there is a towering gold spruce near Port Clements that no one can account for at all—not another tree like it is recorded anywhere.

The road north to Mile 648 on the Alaska Highway covers some 500 miles of British Columbia's most primitive terrain. The Cassiar Mountains comprise one of Canada's most significant volcanic regions, and Tahltan and Tsimshian Indians say that eruptions have occurred here within the past century. More than 30 lava cones can be seen around glacier-rimmed Edziza Peak (Edziza means 'cinders' in the Tahltan language). Near Atlin, British Columbia's most northerly township, the local Tlingit Indians waited eagerly for the annual caribou migration, which provided their winter food supply. They lived in villages on the shores of beautiful Atlin Lake, not far from Whitehorse, in the Yukon Territory. Peaks in the Coast and St Elias Ranges tower to more than 17,000 feet.

The 37,000,000-acre area known as the Peace River Block is traversed by the northern part of Highway 97, which runs through the region that posed such an obstacle to Klondike goldseekers in 1897. They were soon followed by settlers who braved the region's isolation to become prosperous farmers. Northeastern British Columbia has more in common with the prairies than with the rest of the province, and grain is a major crop here. The Alaska Highway has furthered commerce and industry in the area: it begins at Dawson Creek and connects the Peace River country with Fort St John and Fort Nelson.

107 Evergreens of the north woods keep their timeless vigil over the wilderness.

108/109 The wide open spaces near Dawson Creek mark this northerly region of British Columbia as part of the Great Plains.

110 Kayaking in the watertight canoe invented by the Eskimos is a popular sport in ice-bound northern waters.

111 top The steamboat Tarahne is now a museum piece on 307-square-mile Atlin Lake, the province's largest natural lake.

111 bottom Azouzetta Lake in its exquisite Rocky Mountain setting near Chetwynd.

112-113 Oxbow Slough, along the Omineca, is bordered by sweeping stands of spruce.

114 A prosperous, well-kept ranch in northern cattle country.

115 A parish church built of native timber serves as a focal point for community life.

116-117 Kwadacha Wilderness Provincial Park in the northern part of the Rocky Mountains.

118 Hardy sled dogs eat and sleep outside throughout the long northern winter.

119 A trapper's cabin in British Columbia's St Elias Mountains.

120-121 Heavy snow is the rule in the towering Coast Mountains of the north, which have Canada's highest rain and snowfall totals.

122 Northern Canada is a naturalist's paradise, wherein an incredible variety of wild animals can be observed in their natural habitats: (clockwise from top left) a well-insulated mountain goat of the northern Rockies; a dappled fawn awaiting the return of its mother; the rock ptarmigan, which blends imperceptibly into its surroundings; and an alert black bear on the lookout for an intruder into his territory.

123 A stately elk, or wapiti, crowned with magnificent palmate antlers, lifts his head from his browsing on the edge of a northern forest. Roosevelt elk are native to Vancouver Island, but have now been reintroduced to the mainland. Rocky Mountain elk are found in the foothills of the Peace River area and in the Kootenays.

124-125 The rocky headlands of the northerly Queen Charlotte Islands, separated from the Prince Rupert area by Hecate Strait.

126 A motionless seagull is silhouetted by a Pacific sunset.

127 The northerly port of Prince Rupert prospers
through its fishing fleet and forest industries.